Before We Go Back to School

Kristi Dusenbery

Copyright © 2025 Kristi Dusenbery

All rights reserved. This book or any portion thereof may not be reproduced or used in any manner whatsoever without the express written permission of the publisher except for the use of brief quotations in a book review.

Printed in the United States of America

ISBN 979-8-9928228-0-9

The Laughing Grandma
Indianola IA 50125

www.TheLaughingGrandma.com

For every teacher working tirelessly to meet the increasing needs of students.

Thank you ♡

Long before school was ever a thought, Long before lessons ever got taught,

God knew your name.

And he already loved you so much!

So much,
that he gave you
just the right eyes
and just the right nose,
just the right skin
and just the right toes.

He gave you a purpose

and helps you to grow.
He watches your steps
wherever you go.

And now that you're older
and fall's almost here
I can hear **JESUS CHEER**
Cuz he knows that it's time
for a great school year!

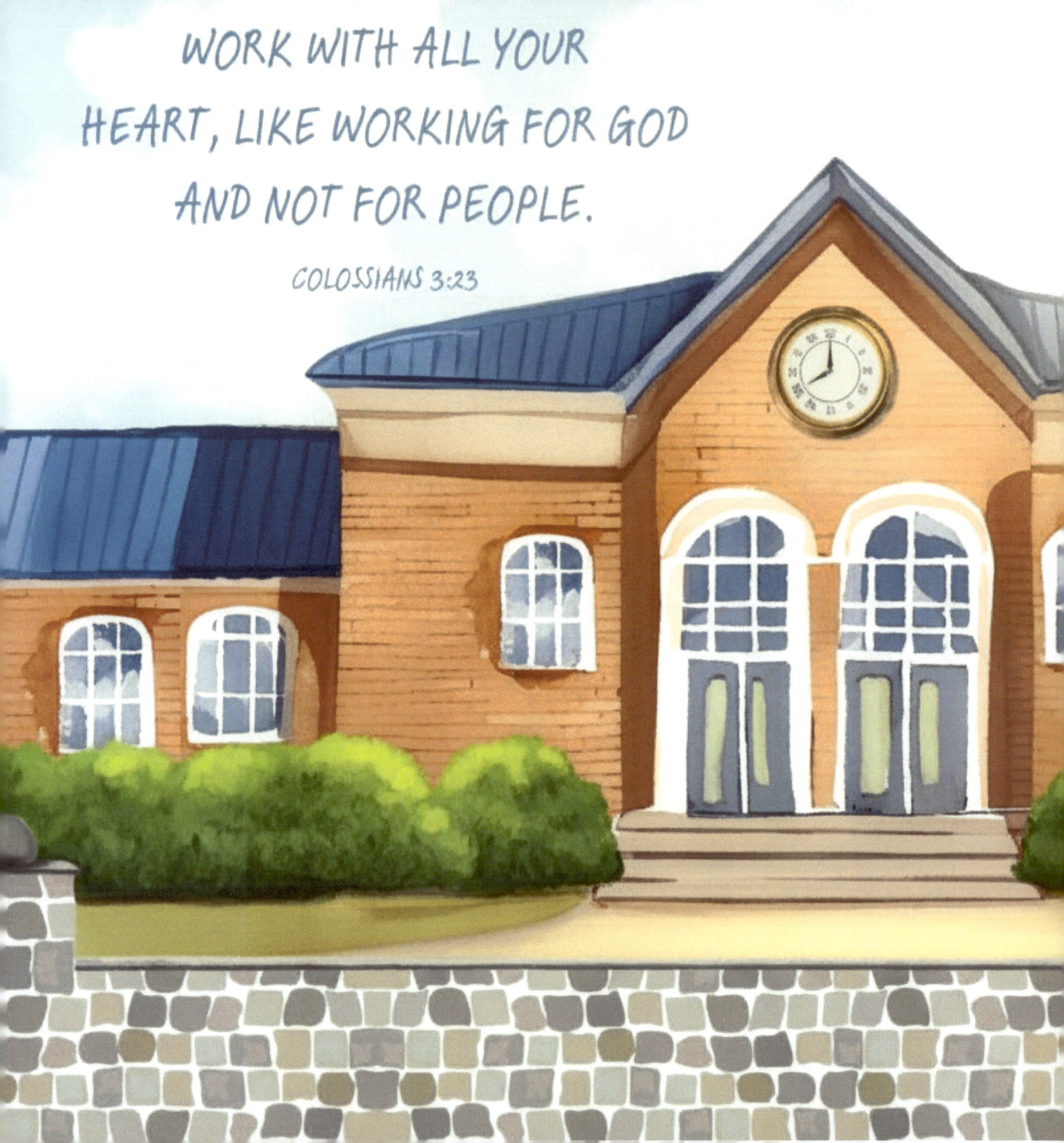

He chose

just the right school

with teachers who care
and new friends to make
   . . . everywhere!

But before you go back
it's important to know,
that school's for more
than just reading and math.
School's much more
than just going to class.

It's a chance to grow up
and practice hard things.
It's a chance to find joy
   . . . in all that it brings!

WELCOME
To Our Class

Jesus said,
"If you LOVE
me you will
DO what
I Command"

John 14:15

KIND

One thing you'll see
when you walk into school
are posters and signs
with all sorts of rules.

Like . . .
- **HANDS TO YOURSELF**
- **LINE UP THE RIGHT WAY**
- **WALK IN THE HALLS**
- **LET EVERYONE PLAY**

And you know what?
When you follow the rules
   by being polite
      and doing what's right,
it shows Jesus you love him
deep down inside.

You'll spend
lots of time learning
　so many facts
about science and history,
computers and maps.

Listen and study

soak up all you can!

Grow wise,
just like Jesus,
so you'll understand
　all that you need
　　for all that God plans.

It won't always be easy
and it might make you doubt,
in who you are
and what life's all about.

But when you're upset
or things seem a mess,
Just look in the mirror
and take a deep breath.

Next,
smile and say:

I'll be okay!

God made me
    and loves me,
and he'll show me the way.

Trust him to use
ALL you go through,
to help you
    grow patience
        and confidence too.

Then way up in Heaven,
far over the moon,
his angels will smile
as they watch your heart

Now, some kids at school
might say some mean things,
making fun of your hair
   or your friends
      or your jeans . . .
Just remember that Jesus
heard mean things a lot!
Some people made fun
of the things that he taught,
**but he never worried
if they liked him or not.**
The only **ONE** Jesus
   tried to impress
      was his Father in Heaven,
         and nobody less.

TREAT OTHERS THE WAY YOU WANT TO BE TREATED

MATTHEW 7:12

You see,
some kids get lots
of love and hugs,
**but the sad truth is
not everyone does.**

Some kids are LONELY
and some are AFRAID.
Some kids feel ANGRY
most of the day.
Some kids are SHY
and some kids are RUDE,
some kids feel ANXIOUS
and some just NEED FOOD.

But, how can YOU help them?
What can YOU do?

You can remember
that God made every kid
and that they have
   a purpose, too.
**He loves each one
to the moon and back,**
just like he loves you.

So, when someone is lonely
   invite them to play.
When someone is angry
   show them some grace.
When someone is worried,
   sad or afraid,
   a few kind words
   could change
   their whole day!

And if there's ever a day
when **YOU** feel alone,
like nobody's there
and you're out on your own,
it's important to know:
    No matter the day
    No matter the time

your Father in Heaven is right by your side.

Just take a big breath
and say a quick prayer.
He hears what you say
    anytime,
        anywhere.

So go back to school
with a smile shining bright.
Remember you're loved
and hold your dreams tight.

spread joy

just like glitter
all through the halls
    and do some good deeds,
        no matter how small.

Cuz God has **BIG** plans
for **YOU**, my sweet child,
and it will be a great year
    full of learning
    and memories
    and so many smiles!

Jesus Loves You So Much

The wrong things you do keep you far from God.

Everybody sins. Sin is when we choose to do, think, or say things that we know are wrong. The Bible says that our sin separates us from God and causes him to turn away from us. Isaiah 59:2

Jesus made a way for your sins to be forgiven.

Jesus chose to die on a cross, to take the punishment for our sins. But he didn't stay dead! God's power caused him to come back to life. Even now, Jesus lives in Heaven and he wants you to live there with him someday. The Bible says that Jesus carried our sins in his body on the cross so we can be healed and filled with joy. 1 Peter 2:24

God wants you to accept his free gift of forgiveness.

To receive his free gift of forgiveness, we can pray and tell God that we are sorry for our sins, we believe Jesus died to forgive us, and that he lives to make us new. The Bible says, if we say out loud that Jesus is Lord and believe in our heart that God raised him from death, then we will be saved. Romans 10:9

Dear God,

I know that I have done bad things and I'm sorry. I believe that Jesus came to earth as a baby, he never sinned, and he died on the cross to forgive my sins. I also believe that he came back to life so I can be forgiven, have joy in my heart, and go to Heaven someday. I want you to be part of my life so I can be in your family. Please help me to do what the Bible says and help me to make good choices every day. Thank you so much!

Amen

Now what?

- Be excited! Jesus has washed away your sin and you are part of his family!
- Read the Bible and ask God to help you make good choices.
- Spend time with other people who are in God's family by going to church.
- Be thankful for every good thing and every good promise God gives you.

Knowing God's Truth

Knowing God's truth helps us grow stronger and wiser when things are hard. Let's think of times when each of these Bible verses might help? Then, memorize them so you will know God's truth when you need it most. It might even help to write the words on cards to carry in your backpack.

"God made Every part of me in an amazing and wonderful way."
(Psalm 139:14) Say this truth when you feel left out, someone teases you, or you wish you were more like someone else.—you are made wonderfully, even when it doesn't feel that way.

God says, "I know the plans I have for you . . . plans to give you hope and a good future."
(Jeremiah 29:11) Say this truth when something goes wrong or you feel really disappointed—God's plan is good even when things feel confusing.

"Work with all your heart, like working for God and not for people."
(Colossians 3:23) Say this truth when there is work to do that you really do not want to do—It makes God happy when we work hard.

"Jesus said, "If you love me you will do what I command."
(John 14:15) Say this truth when you need to make a good choice, like telling the truth or listening to your teacher—even when it's hard.

"Jesus grew stronger and wiser, and God's blessings were with him."
(Luke 2:52) Say this truth as a reminder that mistakes are okay. You just need to learn from them so you will grow stronger and wiser—just like Jesus did.

"I can do all things through Christ because he gives me strength."
(Philippians 4:13) Say this truth when school work, friendships, recess, or sports are hard—God gives you strength to keep trying.

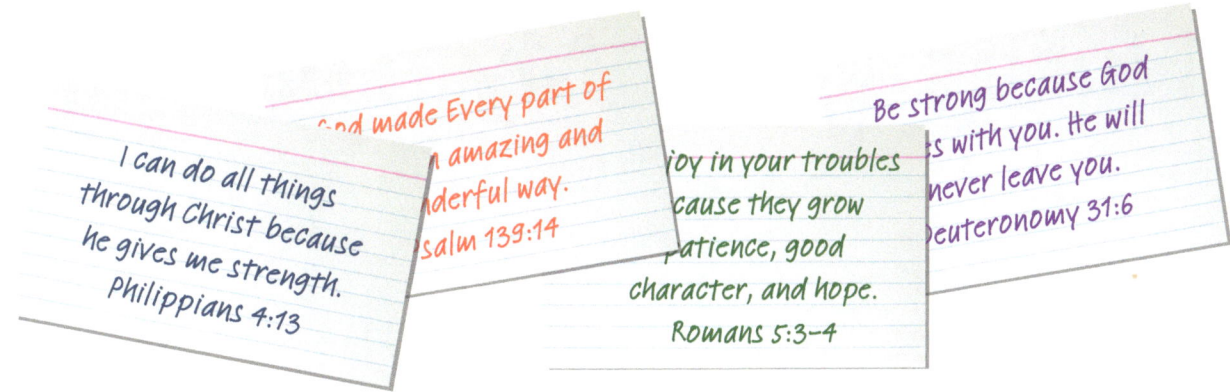

"Find joy in your troubles because they grow patience, good character, and hope."
(Romans 5:3-4) Say this truth when you get a bad grade, have trouble with friends, or get in trouble—God will use it to grow you.

Jesus said, "I try to please the One who sent me."
(John 5:30) Say this truth when someone is trying to get you to do something that you know is wrong—what God thinks of you is more important than what friends think of you.

"Treat others the way you want to be treated."
(Matthew 7:12) Say this truth when you see someone having a hard day or being mistreated by other kids—God can use you to show his love and care for others.

"Do your best to live at peace with everyone."
(Romans 12:18) Say this truth when you don't agree with things that others say or do—sometimes it's more important to be kind than to demand your own way.

"Be strong because God goes with you. He will never leave you."
(Deuteronomy 31:6) Say this truth when you feel homesick, you need to stand up to a bully, or you feel lonely—God is always with you.

"God uses us to spread the joy of Jesus everywhere."
(2 Corinthians 2:14) Say this truth to remind yourself that God uses the light of your smile and kindness to help others to feel his love and joy.

Notes From My Teachers

Notes From My Teachers

Notes From My Teachers

Notes From My Teachers

The Before Books & Activity Books

The Before Books create space for the people you love to encounter the truth that they are deeply loved by the God of the Universe who created them for a beautiful purpose. The activity books provide ways to personalize that message even more. Before rushing into life's special occasions *p-a-u-s-e* to celebrate the joy of Jesus!